THE AMAZING MATH JOURNEY

1

NUMBERS AND COUNTING

Written and illustrated by

Youdao Joyread Editorial Board

Books Beyond Boundaries

ROYAL COLLINS

The Amazing Math Journey
Volume 1: Numbers and Counting

Written and illustrated by Youdao Joyread Editorial Board
Editorial Board Members: Yan Jiarui, Cui Yao, and Wang Dandan
Illustrator: Yan Jiarui

First published in 2024 by Royal Collins Publishing Group Inc.
Groupe Publication Royal Collins Inc.
BKM Royalcollins Publishers Private Limited

Headquarters: 550-555 boul. René-Lévesque O Montréal (Québec) H2Z1B1 Canada
India office: 805 Hemkunt House, 8th Floor, Rajendra Place, New Delhi 110 008

ISBN: 978-1-4878-1170-9

To find out more about our publications, please visit www.royalcollins.com.

THE AMAZING MATH JOURNEY

1

NUMBERS AND COUNTING

www.royalcollins.com

Character Profile

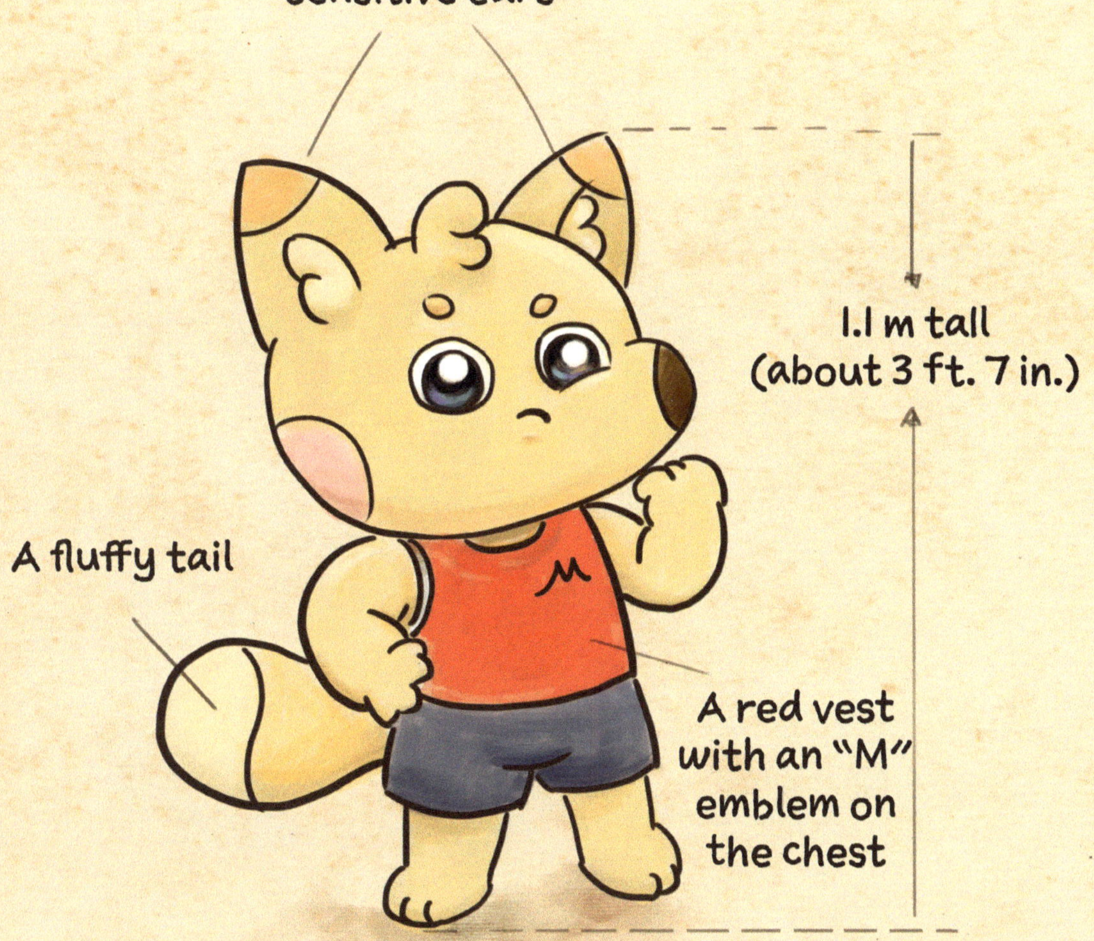

Little Fox

A true fox descendant who lives on the Math Planet. He loves adventure, has a kind heart, and is always curious about the unknown.

Time and Space Travel?

A mysterious force takes Little Fox to

ANOTHER SPACE AND TIME.

Where did Little Fox go?
Who did Little Fox meet?
How will Little Fox get back to the

MATH PLANET?

Everything that happened in that other time and space is recorded here!

QUICK!
Open Little Fox's diary,
solve the riddles,
and find the real **ANSWERS!**

Contents

Little Fox still has classes on the weekends, right?

Little Fox's dad

Yes, this weekend there's a logic analysis class, next weekend there's a spaceship theory class, and the weekend after that . . .

Little Fox's mom

Ugh! With so many classes and so much homework . . .
When can I go out and play?

Mysterious Planet

Location: Math Planet   Weather: Clear

I sat at my desk, feeling dizzy from a morning of homework. Sunlight streamed in through the window in front of me. I looked up and saw the clear sky outside and heard the playful chirping of birds that made my heart long to be outside.

I lied to my parents in order to go out and play, saying I had to ask my teacher some questions. I knew it was wrong, but I was overwhelmed with homework.

I sneaked into the basement and started the spaceship, planning to return within 20 minutes. But there was an accident—a **BLACK HOLE** appeared in the universe! Before I could react, the spaceship and I were sucked into the black hole . . .

"Ah . . ."

I felt myself spinning inside the black hole, spinning . . . then I landed in a dense thicket. Fighting intense dizziness, I found myself in a completely unfamiliar environment. This was not my home, the Math Planet, but an unknown, **MYSTERIOUS PLANET**!

What's even stranger is that my spaceship had **DISAPPEARED**!

How could I get home without the spaceship? I was suddenly panicked and frightened.

What was I going to do?

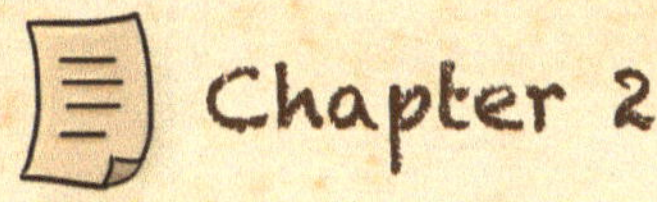

Chapter 2

Magic Patterns

Location: Mysterious planet Weather: Clear

I knew it was too late to regret it now.

"Phew . . ."

I took a deep breath to calm down. I decided to find my spaceship and then hurry back home!

As I walked, I suddenly heard tapping sounds coming from the distance! The sounds stopped and started, and I couldn't make them out with my ears open.

"Could someone have found my spaceship?"

Thinking about the spaceship, I quickened my pace and ran in the direction of the sounds.

The plants here are dense. Anxiously, I pushed through the layers of bushes, only to be disappointed that there was no spaceship behind them. However, to my surprise, on the other side of the river, there was

On the other side of the river, there was a strange man. It turned out that the knocking sounds were coming from him!
Bang! Bang! Bang!
Will he hurt me?
What is he doing here?
Does he know where my ship is?

Even though I couldn't figure out what he was doing, I quietly left to avoid any trouble and to continue searching for my **SPACESHIP**.

Walking along the riverbank, I soon discovered a pile of rocks with patterns not far away.

Who drew these strange patterns?

What do the sun and eye patterns mean?

Primitive Man?

It turns out that this strange person is a PRIMITIVE MAN.

Weapons: stones, sticks, and bones

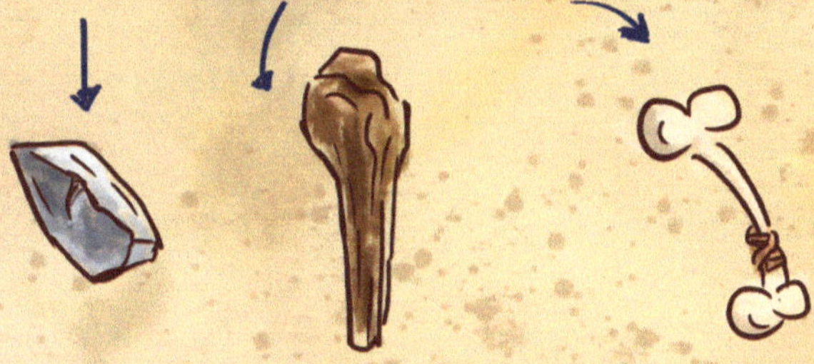

Living by gathering plants and hunting animals

Primitive man's dwelling: CAVES

Human evolutionary timeline:

Hominid

A very long time later

Primitive man

A very long time later

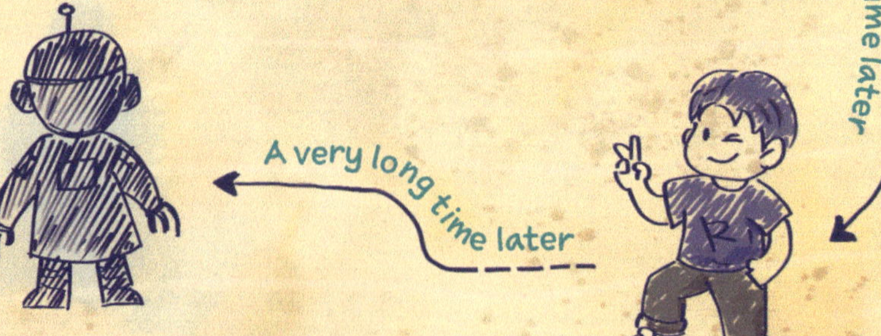

Modern human

A very long time later

Future human

How did primitive man count?

At first, **PRIMITIVE MEN** wanted to figure out how to count, so they tried to count the sun in the sky and found only one sun. To remember the number 1, they used a sun pattern to represent it.

If a primitive man were to say:

I found as many deer as there are **SUNS!**

It would mean he found **1** *deer.*

I found as many birds as there are **EYES!**

It would mean he found **2** *birds.*

Primitive man used the sun pattern to represent 1 and the eye pattern to represent 2. In this picture, can you find any other patterns representing numbers?

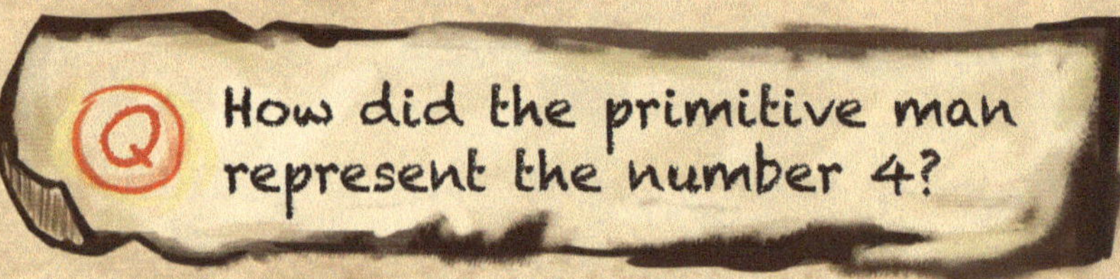

Hint: Find the objects with a quantity of 4 in the picture.

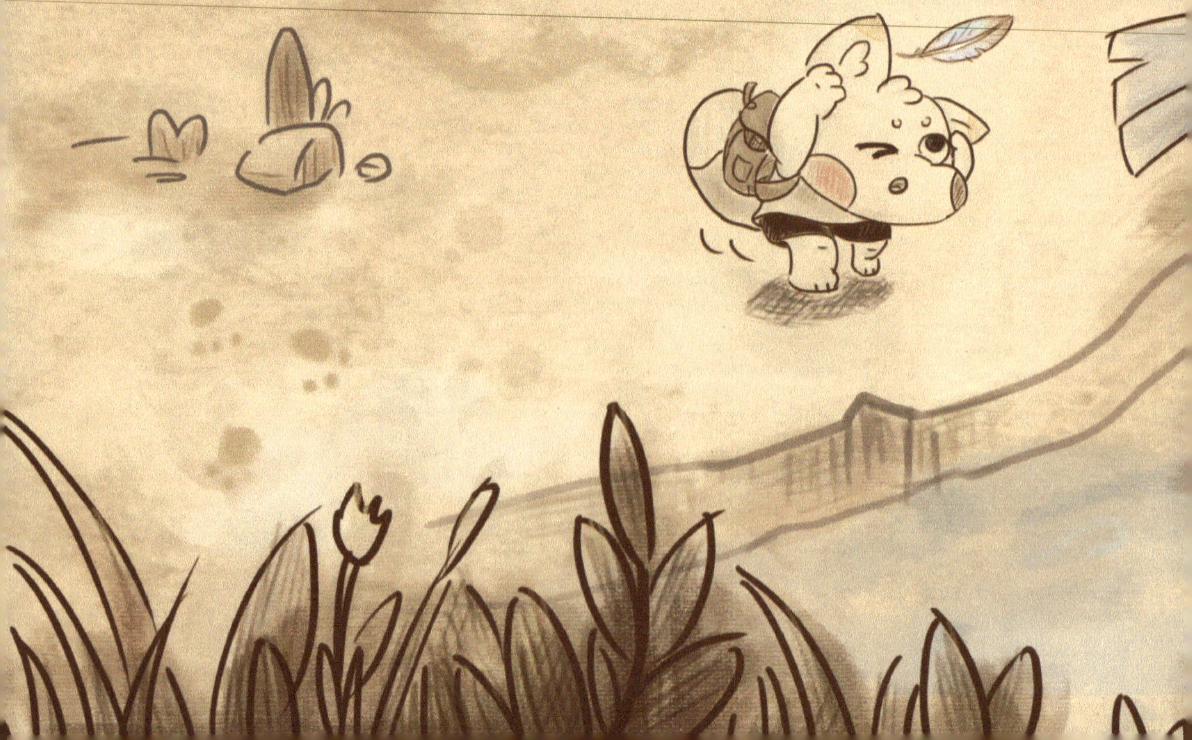

5
Eagle's claws
are so sharp!
1
2
3
4
5
6
7
8

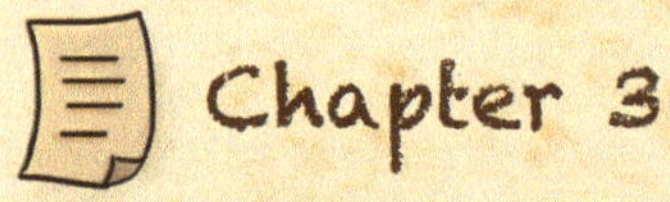

Chapter 3

Strange Knots

Location: Mysterious planet Weather: Clear

I wanted to see similar patterns in other places, so I went around the rocks. To my surprise, behind the pile of stones, there was a **CAVE**!

"What's hidden in this cave? Could my spaceship be inside?"

I thought about this as I slowly approached the entrance.

I poked my head in and looked inside, but the cave was pitch black, and I couldn't see anything.

After a while, my eyes slowly adapted to the darkness, and I could vaguely see the cave's interior.

I held onto the stone wall with one hand while observing the surroundings.

The cave was quite spacious, but what was strange was that many ROPES were hanging in the cave, and each rope had KNOTS tied to it, with each knot looking DIFFERENT from the others.

"What's going on?

What are these knots used for?"

I looked up at the ropes, lost in thought.

Suddenly, there was a sound outside the cave! A figure was gradually approaching the entrance! I didn't have time to react and just stood there, dazed.

There's a **CAVE** behind the rocks!
Why are there so many ropes hanging here?

What are these knots used for?
Who hangs the ropes here?

Fortunately, the person who entered was holding a large pile of corn, which blocked his line of sight, so he didn't notice me. Just as I was thinking about how to escape the cave, my stomach suddenly growled:

"GURGLE ..."

I had no choice but to carefully greet the man. Luckily, he was kind and friendly. Not only did he not drive me out of the cave, but he also gave me a pile of food.

Although I couldn't understand what he was saying, I realized what those strange knots were for by watching him count the corn and tie knots on the ropes. It turned out that the knots were for counting. More interestingly, different colored ropes represented other things!

For example:

YELLOW ropes represent GOLD

WHITE ropes represent SILVER

GREEN ropes represent GRAINS

Who would have thought this person was smart? I suddenly remembered my spaceship. Would he know where my spaceship was?

I drew a picture of a spaceship on the ground, talking and gesturing to him. He suddenly reached out and pointed to the east.

"Can I find my spaceship by heading east?" I asked.

He nodded. I jumped up excitedly, but then he shook his head again . . .

"Huh?" What's going on? Had he seen my spaceship or not?

Knowledge Secret

The Role of Knots

The role of **KNOTS** goes far beyond our imagination. Before using pictures and writing, ancient people began to use knots on ropes to record events.

By looking at the knots they tied, ancient people could recall what had happened at the time. Many numbers in life need to be recorded, such as catching 3 rabbits the day before yesterday, picking 56 pieces of fruit yesterday, and harvesting 200 pieces of corn today . . .

How did ancient people count with knots?

The **ANCIENT INCAS** of **PERU** invented a counting method using knots on ropes called

KHIPU

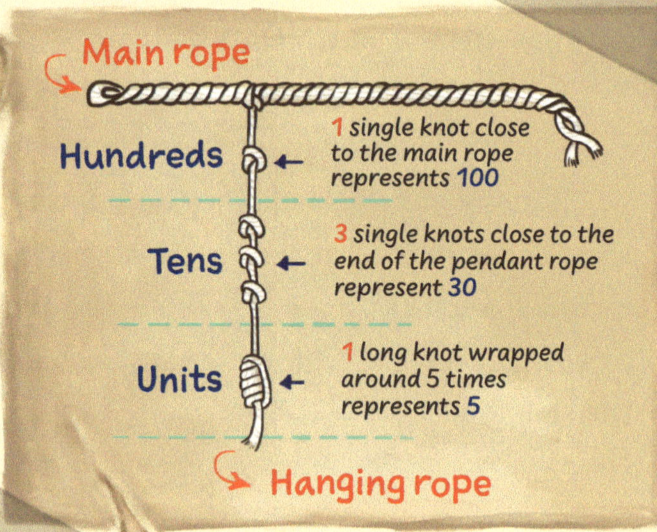

1. Single knot /slip knot

Single knots represent numbers in tens and hundreds, and the number of single knots represents tens or hundreds.

The closer the single knot is to the main rope, the larger the digits it represents. The single knot closest to the main rope represents the hundreds, and the single knot close to the end of the hanging rope represents the tens.

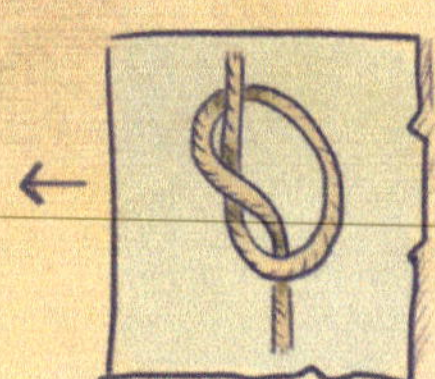

It can represent any multiple of ten.

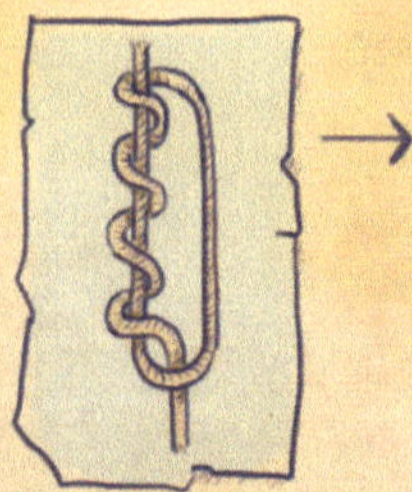

The number of wraps represents the number, which can represent digits 2–9.

2. Long knot

Units are represented by long knots, just a few more wraps based on single knots.

3. Figure-eight knot

The number 1 is unique; a figure-eight knot represents 1.

Focus and observe carefully!

Q Which of the rope below can be tied into a knot?

A

B

C

D

Hint: Try tightening both ends of the rope!

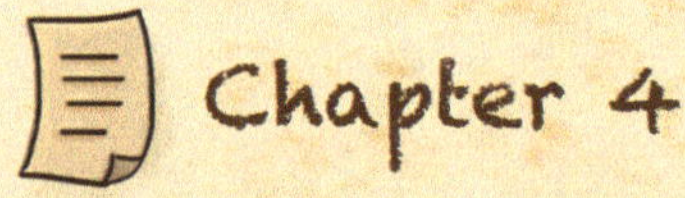

Lotus, Fingers, and Frogs

Location: Mysterious planet   Weather: Clear

I didn't know if the man in the cave had ever seen my spaceship, but there were no other clues.

"Let's go in the direction he pointed and look for clues on the way!" I thought to myself.

So, after saying goodbye to the man in the cave, without hesitation, I began my journey to find my spaceship.

I don't know how long I walked, but I found myself in a DESERT.

The sun was high and hot. I was sweating all over and felt like I might pass out from the heat.

"I wish I could bury myself in the earth! Oh no, in the sand."

But I knew that was an unrealistic thought because the sand beneath my feet was also burning hot.

As far as the eye could see, there was nothing but sand, earth, and a few plants. It was an extravagant hope to find a single patch of shade.

I had an image of sitting at home with air conditioning and having popsicles. As I lost myself in this thought, an intense beam of light suddenly flashed in front of my eyes, bringing me back to reality. Shielding my eyes from the blinding sunlight, I squinted and saw something SPARKLING in the sand not far away!

Ouch! Why is there sand everywhere?
There's not even a bit of shade; it's so hot . . .

Turns out this is **EGYPT**.

I stumbled over to the shiny object and picked it up out of the sand. It was heavy and looked like a KEY.

"What is this? Could it be a treasure?"

As I pondered, I suddenly realized that the sand beneath my feet was sinking, and my body was slowly being SWALLOWED!

"Quicksand? No way! Why am I so unlucky?"

I tried jumping out of the small pit, but I sank even faster! Panicking, I quickly thought of a way to get out of the danger. But before I could come up with a solution, I felt the sand beneath my feet loosen and my whole body fell into the depths of the desert!

Fortunately, it wasn't quicksand, and I found myself in a corridor beneath the desert.

"Finally, a cool place!"

I looked around in relief and noticed that the walls on both sides of the corridor were covered with intricate **PATTERNS**.

"Are these patterns used to decorate the walls?"

Unwittingly, I entered a hall-like area that was spacious and bright, with smooth walls and towering stone pillars reaching to the ceiling. A **SECRET PASSAGE** leading to the depths suddenly appeared on one of the walls.

As I approached, I noticed that the stone slab above the passage was neatly engraved with patterns. While I was absorbed in looking at them, a voice came from behind me:

"Those patterns are hieroglyphs."

Startled by the sudden voice, I turned quickly to see a strange creature with the head of an ibis and the body of a man!

"My name is Thoth," he said.

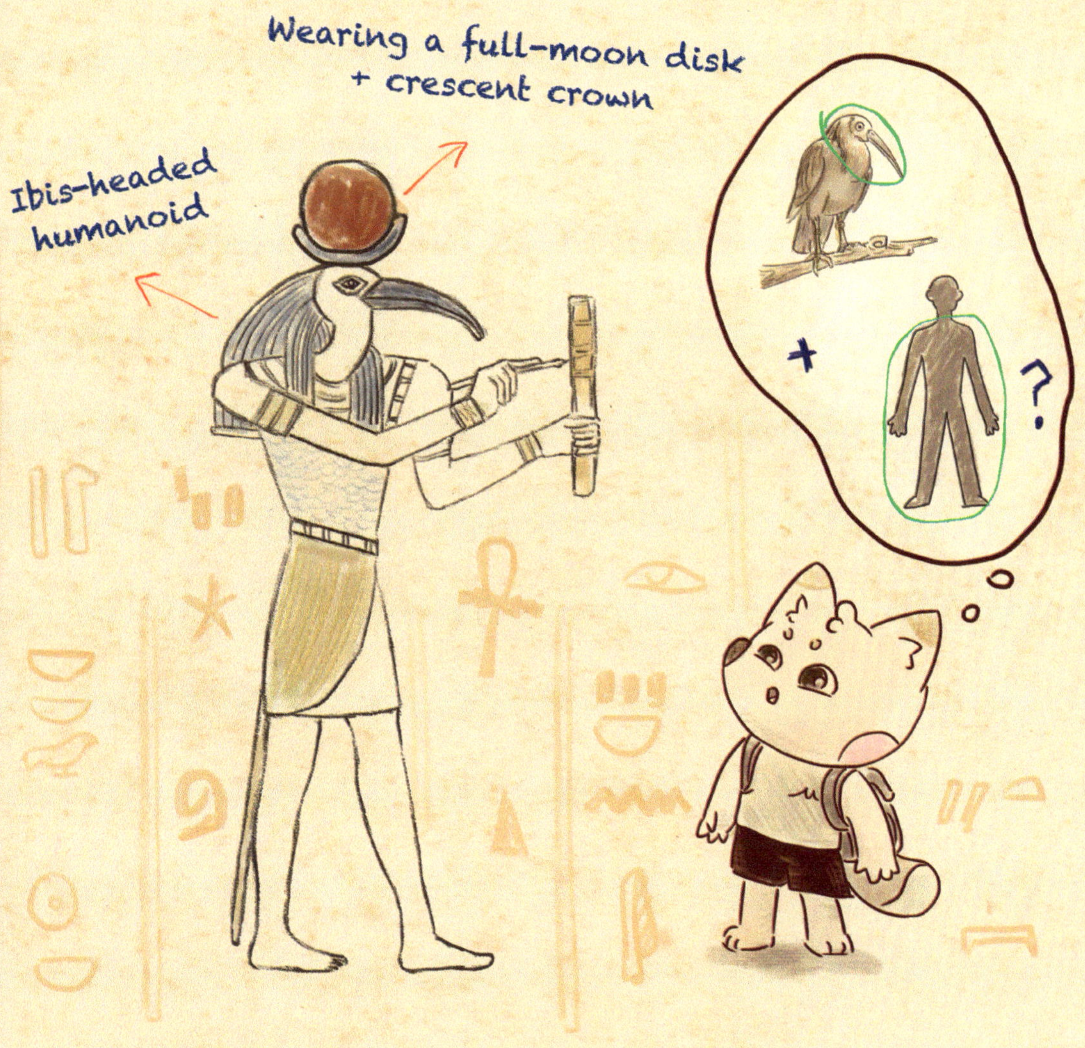

Thoth is the god of wisdom in ancient Egyptian mythology, the god of the moon, mathematics, and medicine, and the legendary inventor of Egyptian hieroglyphs.

I found his appearance amusing but held back my laughter out of respect.

Thoth told me that the patterns on the stone tablet were the **HIEROGLYPHS** (an ancient picture writing) they had invented.

"1 is a single vertical line,
9 is nine vertical lines, 
10 is a piece of rope,
100 is a coil of rope,  
1,000 is a lotus,
10,000 is a finger,  
100,000 is a frog, and
1,000,000 is a person raising both hands . . ."

1 2 3
4 5 6
7 8 9

Thoth went on, but I wasn't interested in their **COUNTING** methods. All I wanted was to find my ship.

Thoth seemed to know what I was thinking, but he didn't tell me where the ship was. Instead, he said,

"Gaining the power of knowledge can help you move in the right direction!"

When I tried to ask for more details, Thoth suddenly disappeared!

"Think carefully and the answer will eventually appear . . ."

His voice echoed through the hall. I walked over to the secret passage and looked down to see the stairs starting from the third step, gradually disappearing into the pitch-black darkness . . .

I rummaged through my backpack and strapped a medallion-like flashlight to my chest. Although its range was limited, it gave me some courage to move forward.

The stairs in the secret passage went UP, DOWN, LEFT, and RIGHT, seemingly never ending.

I wanted to sit down and rest for a moment, but I faintly heard a STRANGE buzzing sound, like a swarm of bees approaching me at high speed!

There was nowhere to hide in the corridor, which consisted only of stairs. The fear of the unknown made my heart race.

"No matter what's behind me, I have to get out of here first!"

So, I ran as fast as possible toward the end of the secret passage.

Knowledge Secret

How did ancient Egyptians count?

In ancient Egyptian **HIEROGLYPHICS***, there were special symbols specifically for representing one, ten, hundred, thousand, and ten thousand. Each time the digit increased, a new symbol was used to express it.*

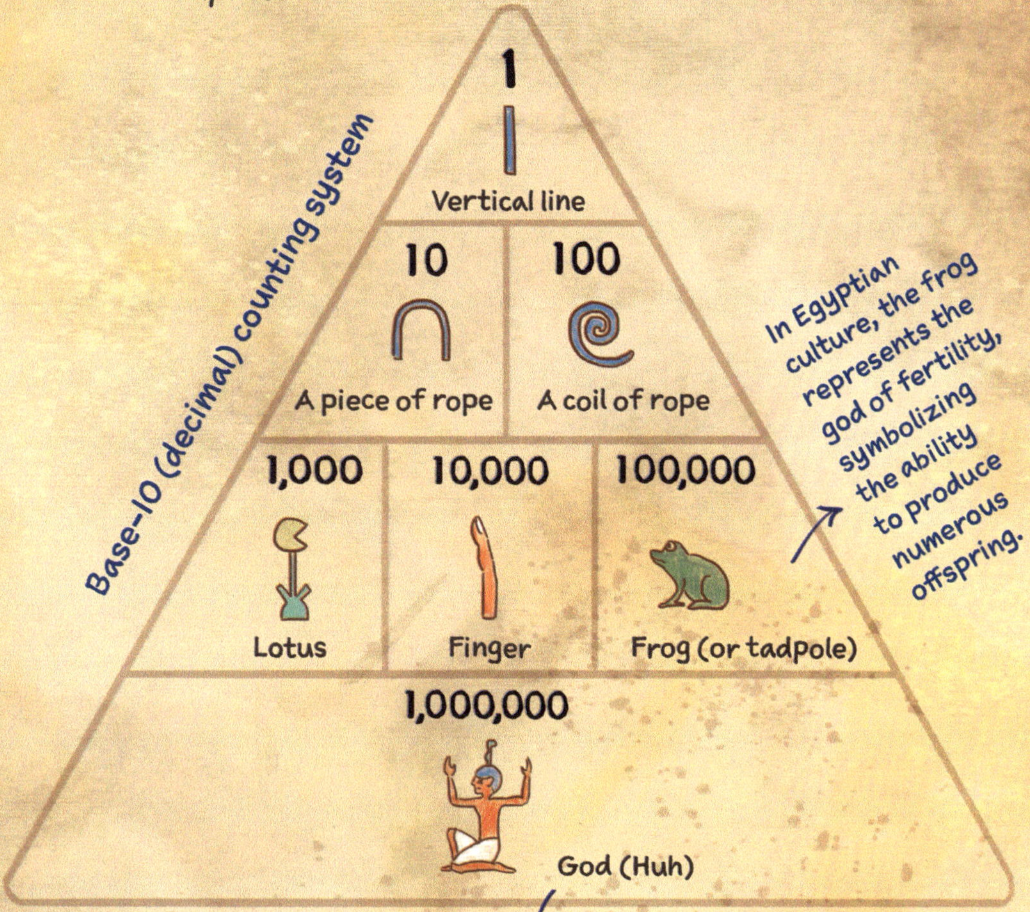

Base-10 (decimal) counting system

1
Vertical line

10
A piece of rope

100
A coil of rope

1,000
Lotus

10,000
Finger

100,000
Frog (or tadpole)

1,000,000
God (Huh)

In Egyptian culture, the frog represents the god of fertility, symbolizing the ability to produce numerous offspring.

"Huh" is the **GOD OF INFINITY** in Egyptian culture.
In the eyes of ancient Egyptians, 1,000,000 was a considerable number.

3
Challenge
Where does this secret passage lead?
What's the number represented by the pattern on the stone slab above the secret passage?

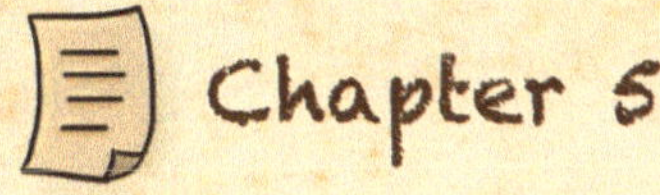

Chapter 5

Shells

Location: Mysterious planet Weather: Fine to cloudy

A small light appeared in front of the secret passage:

"It's the exit!"

I gathered my last bit of strength and ran out of the passage in one breath. At this point, I was completely out of breath. Beside the exit of the secret passage, I bent over, hands on my knees, gasping for air. But the strange sound behind me didn't go away; it was still following me!

I didn't have the strength to run, but fortunately, the dense vegetation surrounding the exit provided excellent cover. Without hesitation, I quickly ducked into the bushes.

Like a swarm of buzzing bees, the strange sound was getting CLOSER to the exit of the passage! The sound was getting LOUDER AND LOUDER.

My heart was POUNDING. I was afraid my heartbeat would be heard, so I held my breath as much as possible.

But just as the sound was about to reach the exit, it STOPPED SUDDENLY . . .

Time seemed to freeze, and the surroundings became UTTERLY QUIET.

I waited longer in the bushes, but there was still no movement.

I slowly emerged from the bushes and looked carefully at the exit of the passage but saw nothing unusual.

"How strange. Am I seeing things?"

I decided it was best to leave quickly!

At that moment, I suddenly realized the vibrant world around me—a dense and green forest where VARIOUS plants grew abundantly, creating a LIVELY atmosphere.

The air was exceptionally fresh, and I couldn't help but take a deep breath, instantly feeling the tension melt away.

I followed the stone steps down to a sinkhole filled with crystal-clear blue water. The plants around the sinkhole were reflected on the surface of the water, shimmering in DIFFERENT COLORS under the sunlight. The sinkhole looked like a DAZZLING blue sapphire. It was truly a sight of remarkable beauty!

I took the foldable bottle from my backpack to fill it from the sinkhole. Just then, water began to gush from the center of the sinkhole:

"Gurgle, gurgle . . ."

The water splashed more and more, and suddenly a **SHELL**-like object appeared, containing a **PERSON**!

"Unbelievable! Someone lives in a shell?"

The shell floated with the water to the shore. To my astonishment, the person inside the shell began to speak:

"Rrrrrrrrrr! I am the guardian god of the Mayan culture: the god of Pawahtun!"

"Oh? Maybe he knows where my spaceship is if he's a god."

Thinking this, I quickly asked him:

"Can you tell me where my spaceship is?"

"Gaining the power of KNOWLEDGE, you will find it naturally . . ."

"The power of knowledge? How can I get it?"

I anxiously stared at him, and he calmly responded, saying with an unhurried tone:

"Continue your journey, observe attentively, engage in thoughtful thinking, and naturally you will obtain . . ."

"Oh . . ."

Upon hearing Pawahtun's words, I was FILLED WIWTH WISDOM. Suddenly, everything became clear, and I gained a deep understanding of it all.

After running in the secret
passage for a long time,
I finally made it out!
The sculptures
here are so strange . . .

For the Maya, shells symbolize water, and life originated from water. So, shells represent growth and resurrection.

The creature that emerged from the shell is the guardian god of Mayan culture,

After thanking the Pawahtun, I gathered my belongings and continued my search for my spaceship.

Along the way, I passed many strange sculptures: snake-headed and bird-feathered statues, giant heads over ten feet tall, and a variety of oddly shaped sculptures, all truly **EYE-OPENING**!

What surprised me the most was the pyramid-like structure. However, unlike a pyramid, it had stairs on each side and a flat top instead of a tip.

"There seem to be patterns on this pyramid!"

I ran over and saw that the patterns on the sides of the stairs were made up of **DOTS**, **LINES**, and **SHELLS**.

"What does that mean?"

I pondered as I walked around the building. Behind the structure was a circular **STONE DISK** divided into three circles. The innermost circle had a human face pattern with the tongue sticking out, the second circle symbolized dots and lines, and the outer circle had various totems.

I noticed that only the second and outer circles could be rotated.

"Could it be that the symbols and totems correspond?"

As I thought, I began to rotate the stone disk. Suddenly, I heard a "**CRACK**" beneath my feet, and the stone disk split open. **CAUGHT OFF GUARD**, I fell into the crack!

How did the Mayans count?

The Maya people used a **BASE-20** (vigesimal) numeral system for counting. In the system, numbers like 80 would be expressed as "4 times 20," and 200 would be described as "10 times 20."

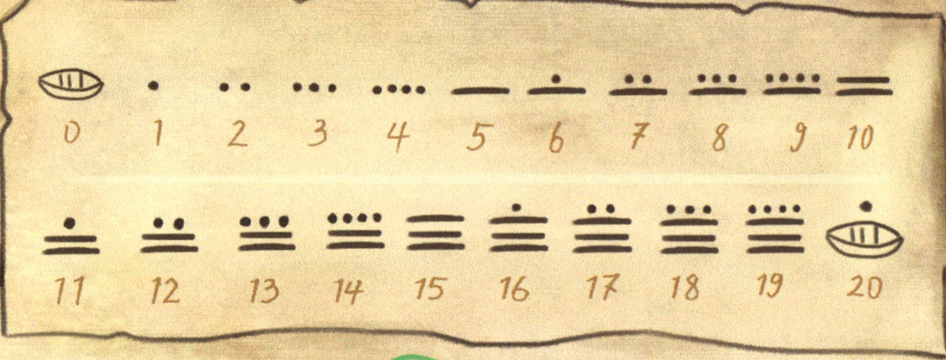

How did the Mayans represent 365?

Note the distance between the two symbols.

The higher the position, the larger the digital order it represents.

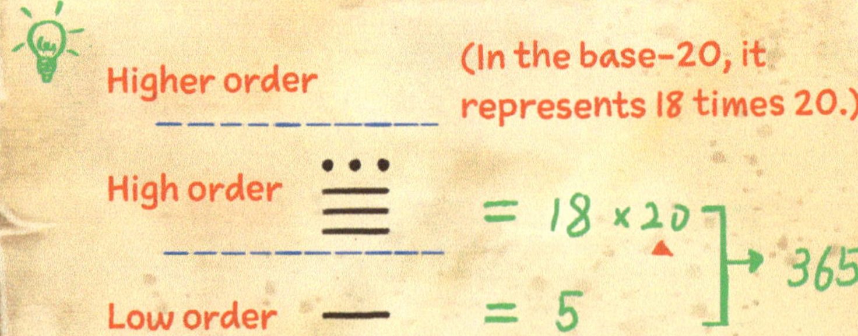

4
Challenge

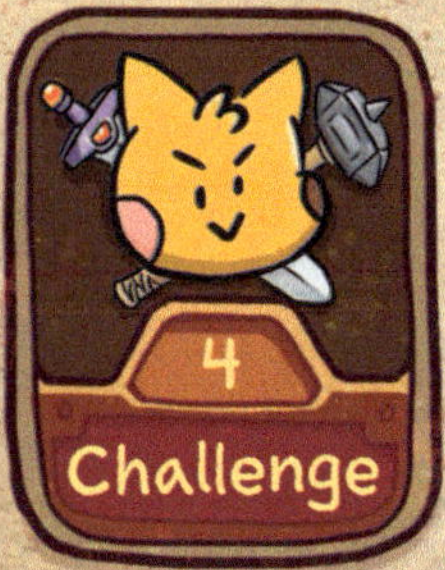

This is the Maya pyramid that Little Fox encountered. From a distance, it looks a bit like the Egyptian pyramids. What do the symbols on the pyramid mean?

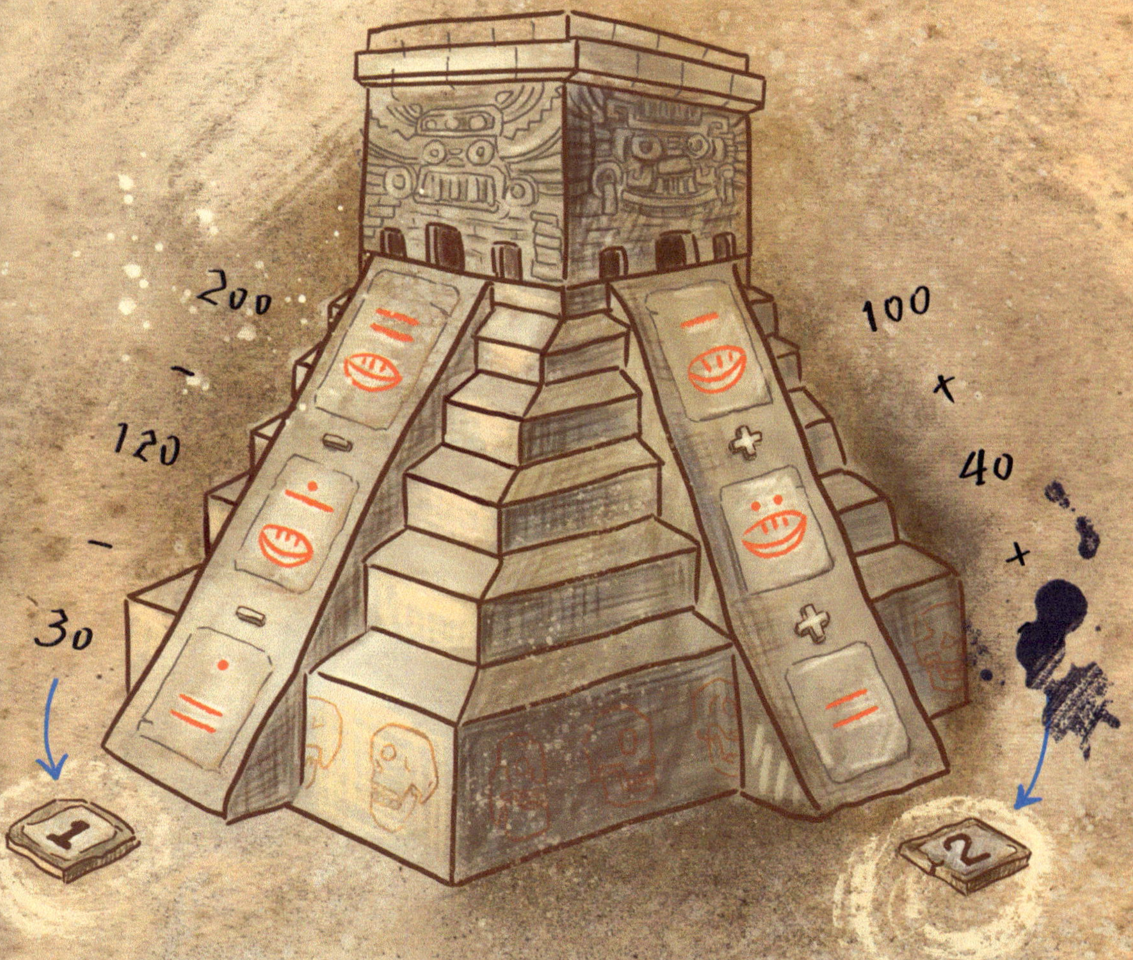
200
-
120
-
30
100
+
40
+
1
2

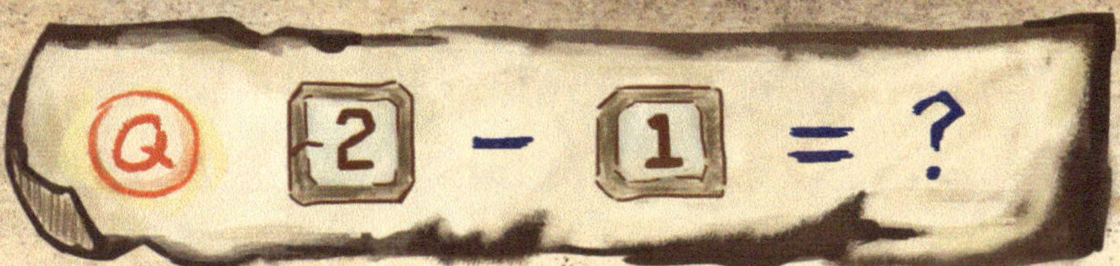
Q 2 − 1 = ?

Hint: Break the puzzle by calculating the numbers corresponding to the digital bricks on both sides of the pyramid and the equation on top.

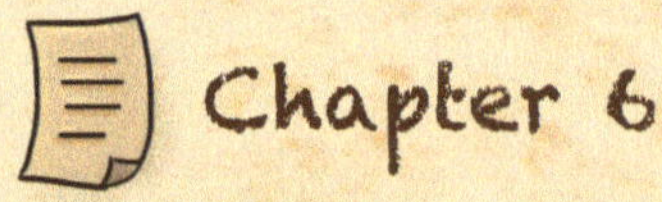

Secret of the Clay Tablet

Location: Mysterious planet Weather: Clear

I fell into a cold and dark **TUNNEL**, spinning around like I was on a **SPIRAL SLIDE**, round and round, all the way down.

The tunnel was smooth and steep, making it impossible to stop!

When I was at a loss, a blinding light suddenly appeared in front of the tunnel, making it difficult to open my eyes. I felt my body "**WHOOSH**" and flew out, and then with a "PLOP," I fell.

After my eyes adjusted to the surrounding light, I realized how LUCKY I was. I had just fallen onto a reed boat on the surface of the water. I would have fallen into the water if I had been a little off!

I got up from the boat and looked at it closely. Although the boat was made of woven reeds, it seemed sturdy and showed no damage or leaks.

I took off my backpack and put it on the boat. At that moment, I felt something under the bottom of the boat. I bent down and reached under the bed.

"It's a clay tablet."

The CLAY TABLET was slightly smaller than the palm of my hand, and SYMBOLS were carved on it. I turned the tablet over and looked at the back. My eyes widened suddenly as a familiar pattern appeared.

"My spaceship? How did it get carved into the clay tablet? Does this tablet have anything to do with my spaceship? And what do these symbols mean?"

The tunnel behind the building led here, and a boat is waiting to take me further!

Papyrus boat: This type of boat is made from bundles of papyrus. Its buoyancy depends mainly on the characteristics of the papyrus itself.

My brain raced, generating a series of questions. After a while, my complex emotions gradually calmed down.

I carefully put the clay tablet in my pocket and decided to find out the meaning of these symbols first. I took the boat and went with the flow of the water.

Sitting in the boat, I suddenly relaxed and my body felt tired. A wave of sleepiness came over me and I yawned repeatedly. Finally, my eyelids drooped heavily, and I fell asleep in the boat.

I don't know how long ago it was, but when I opened my eyes again, I found myself in front of a magnificent building.

Each floor was filled with different flowers, plants, and trees. It looked like a huge, spectacular **GARDEN IN THE SKY** from a distance, which was stunning!

I docked the boat at the shore and walked toward the city gate. In the center of the city, there was a fountain with a stone column covered with dense symbols.

An elderly man told me that this place was **ANCIENT BABYLON**, and these nail- and arrowhead-shaped symbols were their invented script called **CUNEIFORM**.

Looking at these symbols, a flash of light suddenly went off in my head:

"Aren't the symbols on the clay tablet cuneiform?"

Thinking of this, I quickly reached into my trouser pocket, but due to a moment of excitement, the tablet slipped out of my hand and flew toward the fountain.

With a "**PLOP**," the clay tablet fell into the fountain.

"Oh no, there's important information about my spaceship on that tablet!" I was determined to retrieve the clay tablet.

I lay down by the fountain and looked into the water but couldn't see the bottom.

"Is the water that deep? Should I jump in and have a look?"

The Hanging Gardens of Babylon are one of the Eight Wonders of the World.

They used a three-dimensional method of gardening, built on a high platform that rises into the clouds. From a distance, the Gardens were as if it had been created in the sky.

The Gardens were filled with exotic plants from all over the world.

8 Wonders of the World

- Great Pyramid of Giza, Egypt
- Hanging Gardens of Babylon, Iraq
- Temple of Artemis, Turkey
- Statue of Zeus at Olympia, Greece
- Mausoleum of Halicarnassus, Turkey
- Colossus of Rhodes, Greece
- Lighthouse of Alexandria, Egypt
- Terracotta Army of Emperor Qinshihuang, China

WOW!

Hanging Gardens of Babylon

Although I thought so, I took a fish-head-shaped device out of my backpack for safety's sake—a **SIMULATED GILL** that allowed me to breathe freely underwater.

I also covered my gear with a **WATERPROOF BAG**. With everything ready, I dove into the fountain.

After swimming for a while, I suddenly felt something was wrong.

"Is the water too deep? I can't see the bottom! Is the fountain connected to the seabed?"

However, I decided to keep swimming down to find the clay tablet. Even though it was a hot summer, the spring water was ice-cold.

I swam for a while and finally reached the bottom. While searching for the clay tablet, I suddenly felt a **STRANGE FORCE** pulling me backward.

In the dim light, I saw some remains of buildings piled around an arched stone gate. In the middle of the stone gate, a rapidly spinning **WHIRLPOOL** appeared. It was the power of the whirlpool that had sucked me in!

I quickly reached out to grab the nearby water plants, but they were too **SLIPPERY**, and I couldn't hold on.

I **LOST MY BALANCE** and was sucked into the whirlpool along with the fish in the water!

Where do the underwater
building remains come from?

A high-speed whirlpool appeared in the arched stone gate!

How did the ancient Babylonians count?

The ancient Babylonians only needed two symbols for counting:

VERTICAL wedge-shaped mark → 1

HORIZONTAL wedge-shaped mark → 10

Base-60 (sexagesimal) numeral system

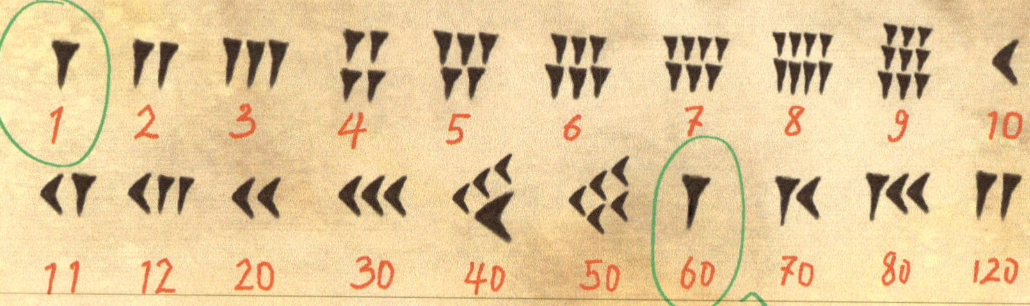

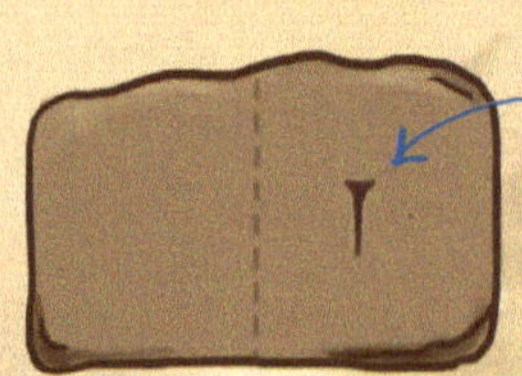
In the low digit, it represents "1."

High digit Low digit

Higher digit	High digit	Low digit
3600	60	1

60 times 60 times

In the high digit, it represents "60."

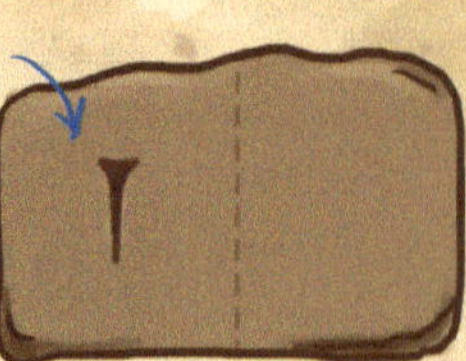

High digit Low digit

Why did the ancient Babylonians use a base-60 counting system? The reason might be related to fingers.

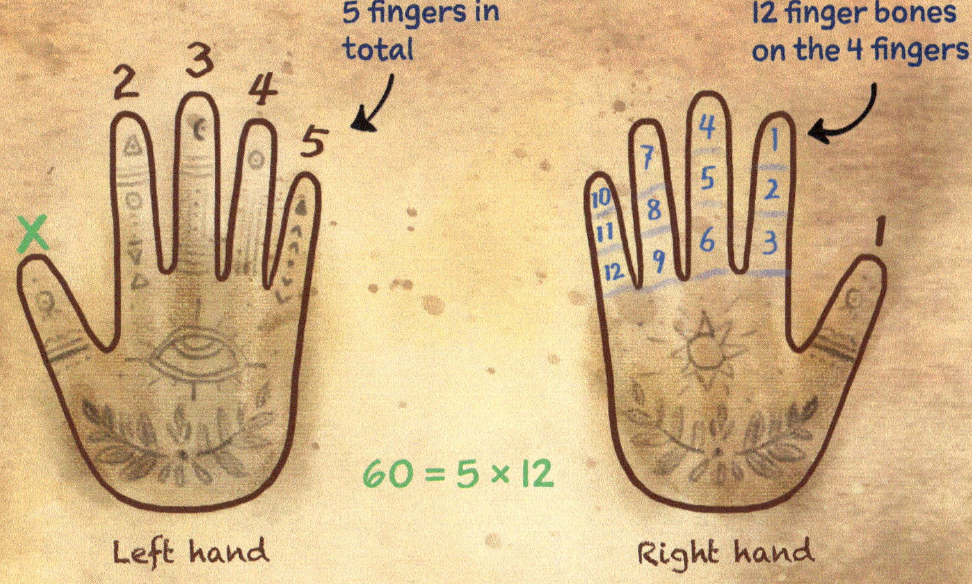

Note: The thumb has a unique role!
It can touch the joints of each of the other 4 fingers.

First, use the right thumb to count the 12 joints on the right hand, then bend the left thumb and lean the joints again. Since there are 5 fingers on one hand, this process is repeated 5 times, allowing one to count to 60.

Why is it called cuneiform?

Cuneiform, also known as NAIL HEAD-SHAPED WRITING or ARROWHEAD-SHAPED WRITING.

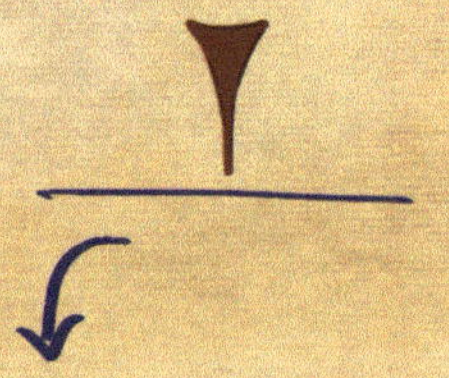

Vertical, nail-shaped

Horizontal, arrowhead-shaped

The English term "cuneiform" is derived from Latin and is a compound word comprising two words.

cuneus + forma = cuneiform
(wedge-shaped)

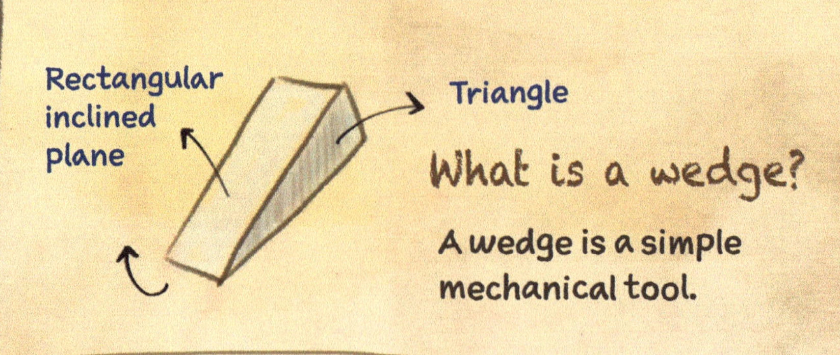

What is a wedge?

A wedge is a simple mechanical tool.

ANCIENT BABYLON *was in the Mesopotamian plain, where wood was scarce, and stone materials were rare. Under the impact of the Euphrates and Tigris Rivers, a large amount of* **CLAY** *was deposited here. Therefore, the Babylonians used clay tablets as writing materials.*

The clay here is different from other regions, with strong adhesiveness.

What is the purpose of a clay tablet?

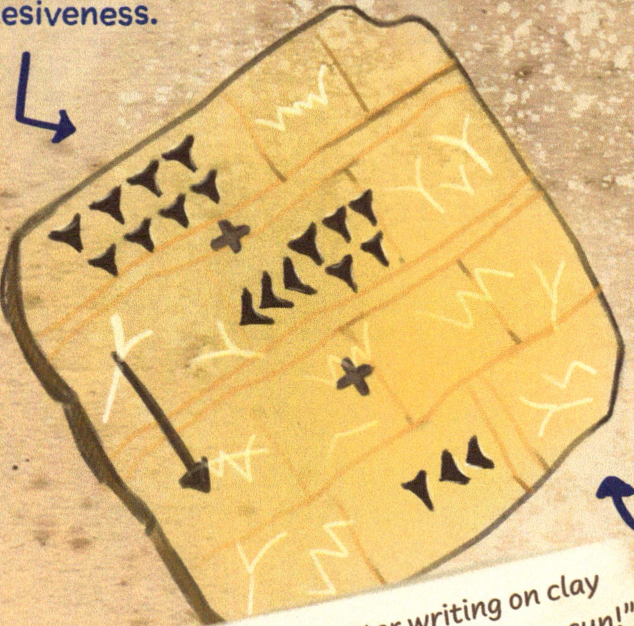

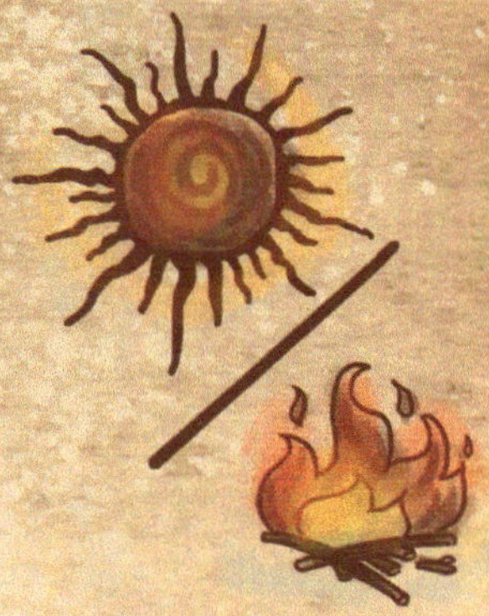

The sturdy "clay tablet books" can be preserved for a long time by drying the written clay tablets in the sun or baking.

"Those who master writing on clay tablets will shine like the rising sun!"

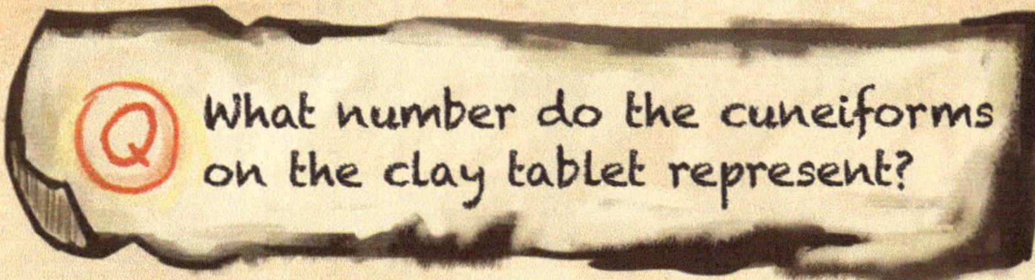

Hint: Solve the puzzle by calculating the equation on the clay tablet.

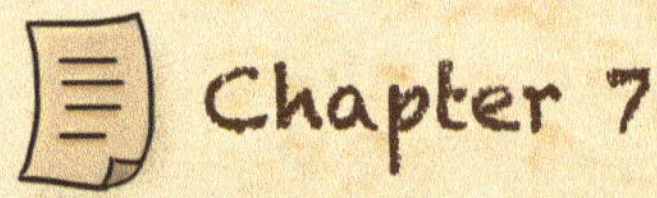

Letters or Numbers?

Location: Mysterious planet   Weather: Clear

I spun around in the whirlpool like a spinning top out of control, the intense dizziness making my mind go blank . . .

After a while, the spinning slowed down and finally stopped, making the environment calm again. I struggled to open my eyes and vaguely saw something brown buried in the sand at the bottom of the water.

"Could it be the clay tablet?"

I swam over, picked up the object from the sand, and discovered that it was not a clay tablet, but a COPPER COIN! At that moment, the dizziness in my head hadn't completely disappeared, and my body was a bit tired. I decided to swim to the surface and rest for a while.

I swam up in one breath, and the moment I surfaced, I immediately noticed something unusual. The well had completely changed, and the surroundings were completely different!

"Where am I?"

Above the water was a petal-shaped double-layered fountain with four LIFELIKE sea monster statues with snake bodies and fish heads inside.

I climbed out of the water, shook off the water on my body, sat down by the fountain, and looked down at the copper coin in my hand. The front of the coin was engraved with some symbols that looked like LETTERS; the back had a picture of an archway, and inside the archway was even a picture of a SPACESHIP!

Drying

Where is the archway on the back of
the copper coin? Is my spaceship there?

It's completely different from the previous fountain! The environment too!
L M X D C I
Do those letters on the coin have special meanings?

"Is my spaceship in this archway?"

I quickly looked around and found that there were many archways.

"It seems I have to find out the meaning of the letters on the coin first!"

Thinking about it, I walked toward the city. Here I met a kind-hearted person who told me that this place was Rome, and the letters on the coin were **ROMAN NUMERALS** invented by the Romans.

"One 'I' is 1, two 'I's are 2, one 'V' is 5, one 'X' is 10 . . ."

"Wait a minute, if one 'I' represents 1, can't five 'I's represent 5?"

I suddenly interrupted him, but he didn't get angry. Instead, he raised one hand, closed his five fingers together, and then separated his thumb from his other fingers, forming a "V" shape.

"One hand has five fingers, so we use 'V' to represent 5," he explained.

I was about to ask him more about the specific meaning of these letters when suddenly a loud noise came from a distance. In the blink of an eye, a knight led a group of soldiers and rushed to my front.

"Take him away!" The knight looked at me coldly and motioned to the soldiers behind him.

"Yes!" Two soldiers answered in unison and bound me with iron chains without explanation.

"Hey! Hey! You got the wrong person!" I shouted at the knight.

"I can give you a chance. Determine your fate in a duel! Hmph . . ." The knight sneered coldly. Ignoring my question, he kicked the horse's belly and turned away.

I was captured like this and dragged by the soldiers to a massive circular building with many archways.

"Welcome to the COLOSSEUM!" The soldier said emotionlessly. So, this was the ancient Roman Colosseum, and at that moment, the roar of ferocious beasts could be heard from inside the arena.

"Ah . . . Will I have to fight a tiger in a duel? I . . . I . . . I'm most afraid of . . . tigers . . ."

As I stood in front of the Colosseum, the roar of the ferocious beasts filled my ears, making me feel so small and helpless that I couldn't help but shiver all over.

As my eyes swept over the rows of archways, I suddenly noticed that each archway had a flat Roman numeral carved above it!

"Could the Roman numerals on the copper coin correspond to the numerals above the archways? I must find a way to get a closer look!"

I planned in my mind and yelled at the two soldiers,

"Hey! I . . . I must go to the bathroom!"

While they were off guard, I broke free of the chains and ran out!

"Stop! Stop!"

The soldiers chased me relentlessly. I ran to the archways, but my ship was not in them.

I stood helplessly in one of the archways, my heart racing and beads of sweat forming in my palms.

"Quickly! Quickly! Over here!"

The soldiers behind me were closing in!

"What should I do?"

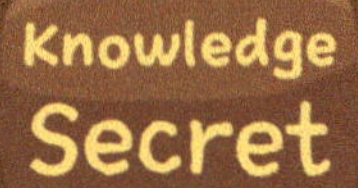

Origins of V and X

L = 50

X = 10

M = 1,000

I = 1

V = 5

D = 500

C = 100

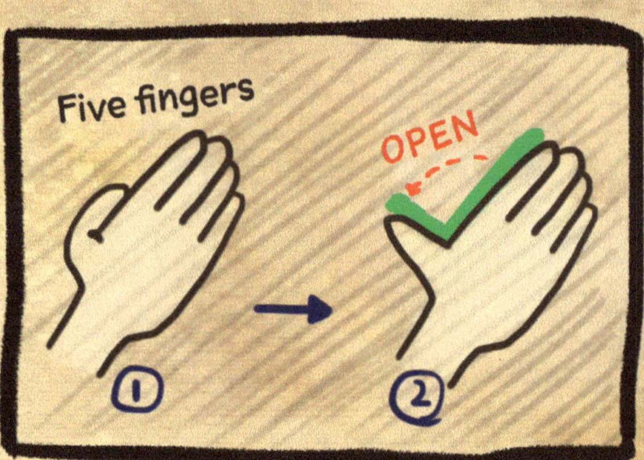

Origin of "V":

Bring the five fingers together, then separate the thumb from the other fingers. Observe the shape of the hand at this point.

Origin of "X":

Combine two "V", then turn one upside down to form an "X."

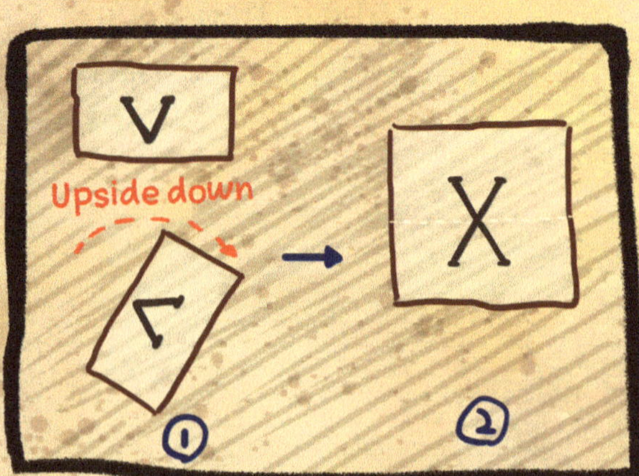

Roman Numerals

1	2	3	4	5	6	7	8	9	10
I	II	III	IV	V	VI	VII	VIII	IX	X
20	30	40	50	60	90	100	500	1,000	
XX	XXX	XL	L	LX	XC	C	D	M	

Ancient Romans invented only **7** symbols, but they could record all numbers. This is because they cleverly used **addition and subtraction**.

Examples:

V + I → VI

Add an "I" to the right of "V" to represent 6:

5 + 1 = 6

V - I → IV

Subtract an "I" from the left of "V" to represent 4:

5 − 1 = 4

6
Challenge
Q
Which archway corresponds to the number 67?
IX
XI
VI
IV
II
LXXV
LXIX
LXVII
XLII
XX
L
V
C
X
LV
LI
LIV
XXX
So many archways.
What secrets are hidden inside?

ROMAN COLOSSEUM

The Colosseum, also known as the amphitheater or arena, is in Rome, the capital of Italy.

This was once a place where ancient Roman Empire's slave owners, nobles, and free citizens watched animal fights or slave duels. It was also a symbol of ancient Roman civilization.

The outer wall is about 57 m (187 ft.) high, almost equivalent to the height of a modern 19-story building. There are 80 archways on the ground floor, a 4-story structure, and an underground basement.

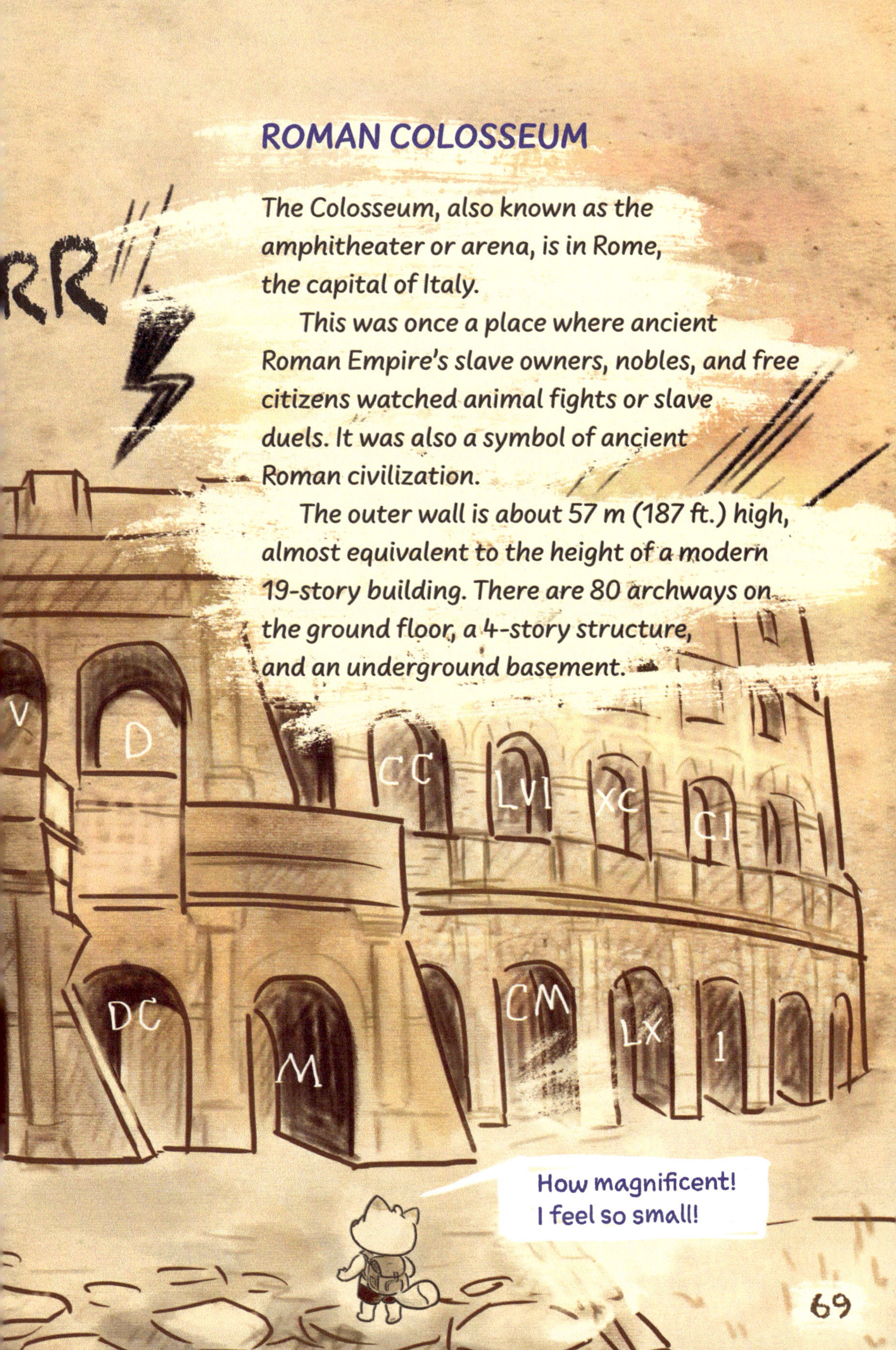

Magic Sticks

Location: Mysterious planet Weather: Fine to cloudy

I remind myself to stay **CALM**!

Inside the archway, I watched carefully again. Suddenly, I noticed an inconspicuous circular groove on the wall to the right of the entrance. Without thinking, I placed the copper coin in the groove, and to my surprise, the coin fit perfectly!

The coin emitted a blinding white light that instantly lighted up the entire archway. The light was so bright that I couldn't open my eyes, and the noise of the soldiers behind me gradually faded away . . .

When I opened my eyes again, the HAIR-RAISING Roman Colosseum was gone, and I was standing on a square platform.

The sun rose between the mountains, and its gentle rays warmed my face. I couldn't help but open my arms and felt the WARMTH all over my body . . .

Suddenly I remembered the spaceship pattern on the copper coin.

"So . . . my spaceship is here?"

I squinted and looked around, vaguely seeing SMOKE rising from a place at the foot of the mountain. I felt that the smoking place might have clues about the spaceship!

So, I quickly descended the mountain and ran in the direction of the smoke.

This place is said to be one of the most mysterious countries on this planet—

the Eastern ancient state

Mount Li

Located in Xi'an City, Shaanxi Province, in China, with an altitude of 1,302 m (about 4,272 ft.). Due to its lush and beautiful scenery, it is also called "Beautifully Patterned Hill."

A beacon tower is an ancient platform for sending messages through light beacons. When enemies invade, smoke would be sent during the day and fire at night, connecting the towers to facilitate message transmission.

In no time I arrived at the smoking place.

It turned out to be a **KILN** where **POTTERY FIGURINES** were made, and the thick smoke came from it.

Many people were working inside and outside the kiln. To be on the safe side, I secretly climbed up a nearby tree to observe the situation.

I saw a person sitting at a table in the corner of the kiln, taking out a **SMALL BAG** from his body. He was talking to himself as he took out many **SMALL STICKS** of the same size:

"One stick represents 1, two sticks represent 2, three sticks represent 3 . . . four sticks . . ."

The man fiddled with the sticks on the table, sometimes laying them horizontally, sometimes vertically. Just as I became absorbed in watching, suddenly a loud noise came from far away!

A soldier, covered in dust, rushed over and saluted the man fiddling with the sticks.

"Re . . . Report! An unidentified object with a strange shape fell into the pit and damaged many pottery figurines!"

"Oh? A strange unidentified object? Could it be my spaceship?" I silently said to myself in my heart.

I wanted to get closer to listen, but my hand slipped, and I fell from the tree, landing right on a pottery figurine below!

The figurine wiggled and fell onto another one next to it, which then fell onto another . . .

"**CLANG! CLANG! CLANG!**" The pottery figurines fell like dominoes . . .

"Oh no . . . my pottery figurines . . ."

The heartbroken man almost burst into tears as he looked at the damaged figurines. Then his face

turned serious, and he pointed at me and yelled at the soldier:

"Catch him! Don't let him get away; bring him back to me!"

"Yes!"

Seeing that the situation is getting worse, I turned and ran, shouting as I go:

"S—O—R—R—Y! I—didn't—mean—it!"

Although it's wrong to run away after **CAUSING TROUBLE**, I didn't want to miss the opportunity to find my spaceship. The unidentified object the soldier mentioned could be the spaceship, so I immediately headed toward the location of the loud noise.

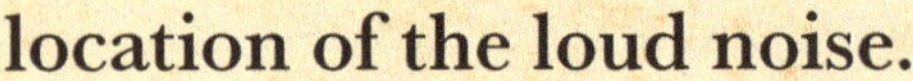

In a short time, I arrived at the edge of a large pit where thousands of life-size pottery figurines were neatly arranged like a huge ARMY. It's a magnificent sight!

However, there's a cloud of dust in the center of the pit, and some of the pottery figurines around it were broken. Through the dust, I vaguely saw the outline of a massive object. Even though the dust had not completely cleared, I recognized it immediately:

"It's my spaceship!"

Excited, I ran toward the center of the pit, my heart thumping with thrill.

How did Ancient Chinese people count?

Ancient Chinese people invented a counting tool called **COUNTING RODS**. People would carry around more than 270 uniformly sized small sticks in a cloth bag attached to their waist. When they needed to count or calculate, they would take them out and place them on a table, bed, or ground, manipulating them according to rules.

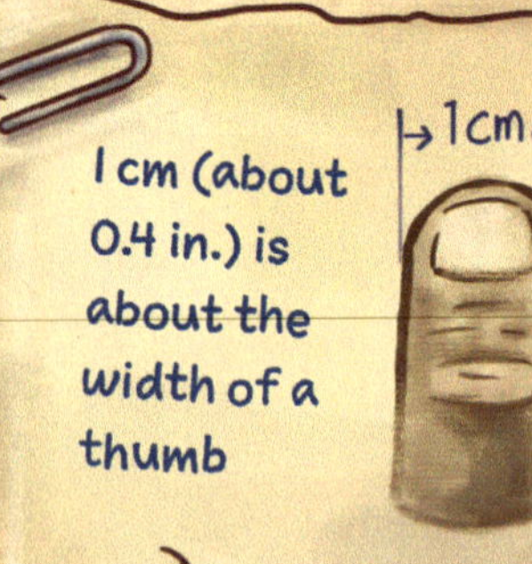

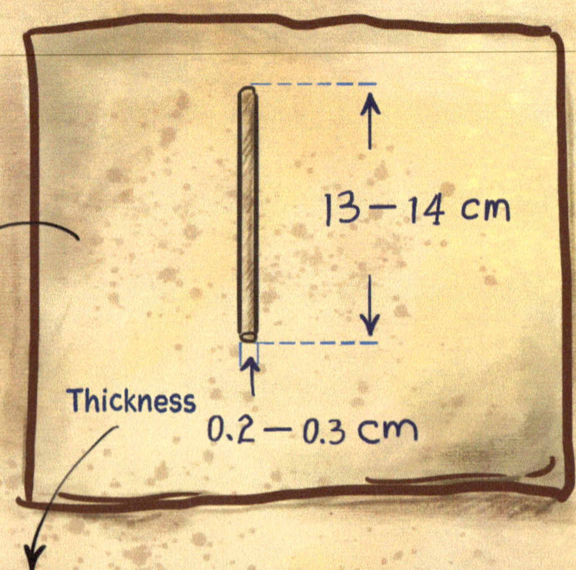

The sticks are generally 13–14 cm (about 5.1–5.5 in.) long, with a 0.2–0.3 cm (about 0.08–0.12 in.) diameter.

Material: Mostly made of bamboo, wood, animal bones, ivory, metal, and other materials.

Two different ways of arranging

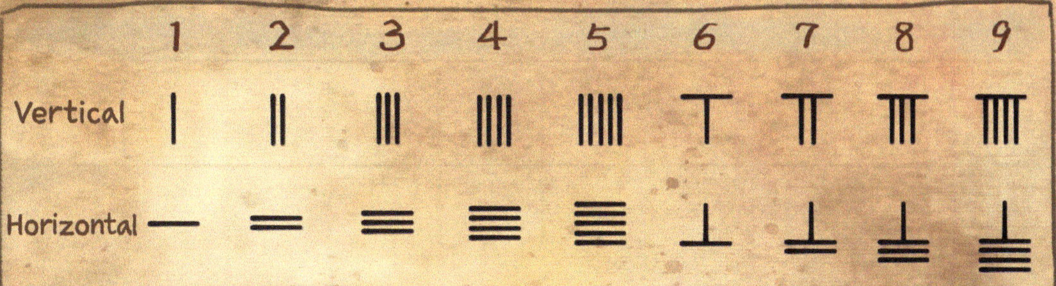

Base-10 system

Why are there two different ways of arranging?

As shown in the table below, the digits increases from small to large from right to left, alternating vertically and horizontally. By following this pattern, any natural number can be represented using counting rods.

The alternating arrangement of the digits allows for clarity and misplacement.

Left ← Right

...	Horizontal	Vertical	Horizontal	Vertical
...	Thousands	Hundreds	Tens	Units

"In the method of calculation, one must first recognize the positions: one vertical, ten horizontal, a hundred to a thousand, a thousand and ten looks at each other, ten thousand and a hundred are equal."

—*Sunzi Suanjing*, a mathematical study from the 4th to 5th century

The ancient Chinese decimal system of counting rods *is one of the most incredible inventions in the history of world mathematics.*

7
Challenge
Q
What number do the sticks on the table represent?
From which directic
should we look?
Left or right?

Knowledge Secret

How many steps are involved in making terracotta warriors?

① Roughly shape the shape of the head, body, and limbs.

② Finely carve the facial features, clothing patterns, and other details.

③ Assemble and connect the finished body parts.

After firing, color the pottery with natural mineral pigments.

Place the completed pottery figurines in a kiln for firing at the temperature of about 1,000°C–1,050°C.

Chapter 9

Journal

Location: Mysterious planet   Weather: Cloudy

I ran out of breath to the ship. Thinking about going home soon, a warmth flowed from the bottom of my heart.

"St . . . stop!"

The shouts of the soldiers behind me interrupted my thoughts.

I quickly pressed the hidden button on the ship and crawled quickly into the opening hatch.

I sat down in the cockpit and quickly started the spaceship.

The spaceship slowly lifted off the ground, and as the energy gathered, it emitted a blinding white light. In the blink of an eye, the spaceship disappeared from the sky.

Fortunately, the spaceship had the LOCATION of the Math Planet, and I finally made it home safely. I parked the spaceship in the basement, and then eagerly ran into the house.

"Dad, Mom, I'm back!" I exclaimed excitedly. I fell into my mother's arms, HAPPY to be home!

But before I could enjoy the warmth of home, that moment of happiness was interrupted . . .

"Did you go ask your teacher about the problem? It's only been five minutes and you're back?" Mom looked at me, confused.

Hearing my mother's words, I was stunned.

"Five minutes? Did all the time I spent traveling, going through hardships, only take five minutes on the Math Planet?"

I made up an excuse and hurriedly hid in my bedroom. I sat blankly at my desk; my mind full of **DOUBTS**.

I felt that this mysterious journey was not easy; it must have some secrets! I took a blank **JOURNAL**

from the drawer and recorded the events of the journey . . .

"Magical patterns, strange knots, frogs, shells, cuneiform writing, Roman numerals, counting rods . . .

What's the connection between these adventures?"

As I was thinking, sleepiness washed over me, and I fell asleep on the table.

In my half-asleep state, I heard a **STRANGE SOUND** that seemed familiar.

I forced my eyes open, and in a daze, I saw a round object floating in the air, emitting a mysterious blue-green light . . .

"Am I dreaming? Or is this an illusion?"

How do modern people count?

Nowadays, the numbers we often use are called **ARABIC NUMERALS**, consisting of 10 counting symbols: 0, 1, 2, 3, 4, 5, 6, 7, 8, and 9.

1. In the early 9th century, the Ancient Arab mathematician Al-Khwarizmi published *Indian Arithmetic*, detailing this decimal counting system from India.
2. Famous Italian mathematician Fibonacci introduced it to Europe.
3. In the 14th century, **Chinese printing technology** spread to Europe, accelerating the promotion and application of Indian numerals, which eventually spread these counting symbols worldwide.

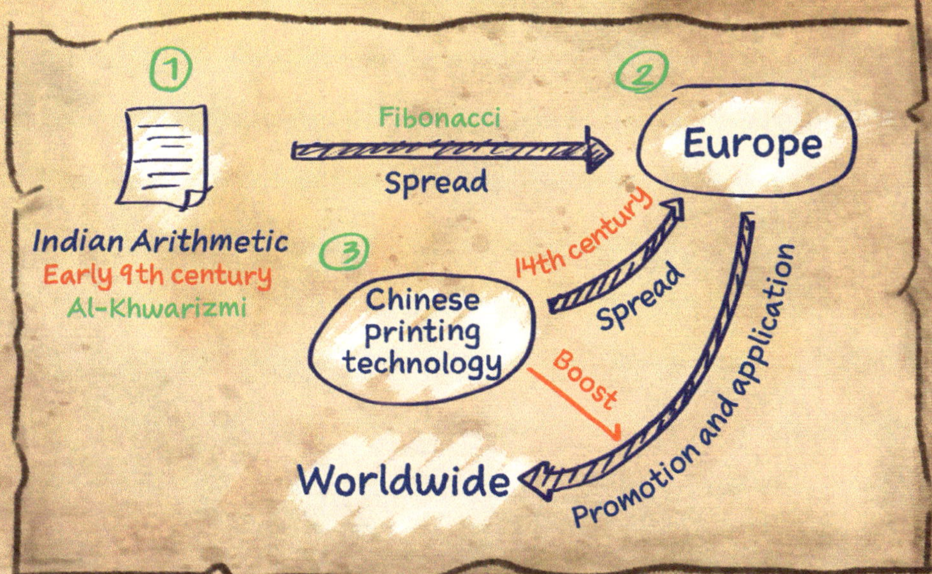

The original Arabic numerals looked like this:

1 2 3
4 5 6
7 8 9
0

The number of angles on the digits surprisingly corresponds to the value they represent!

After a long evolution, they have become what we write today:

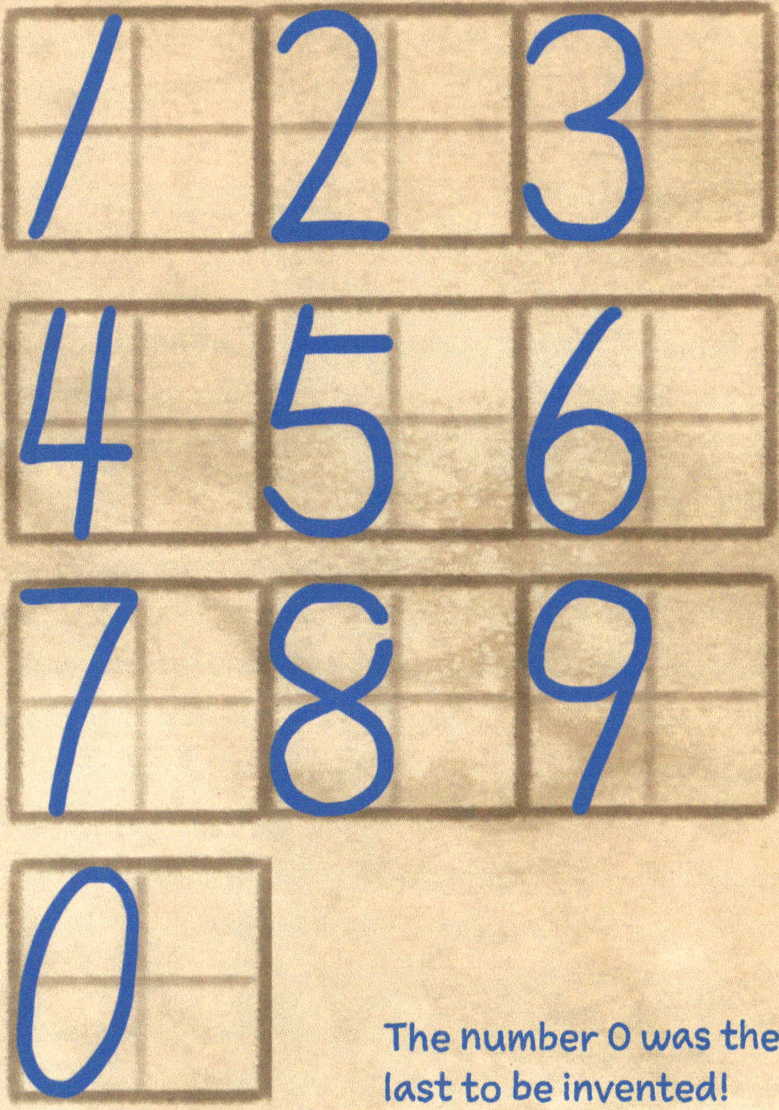

1 2 3

4 5 6

7 8 9

0

The number 0 was the last to be invented!

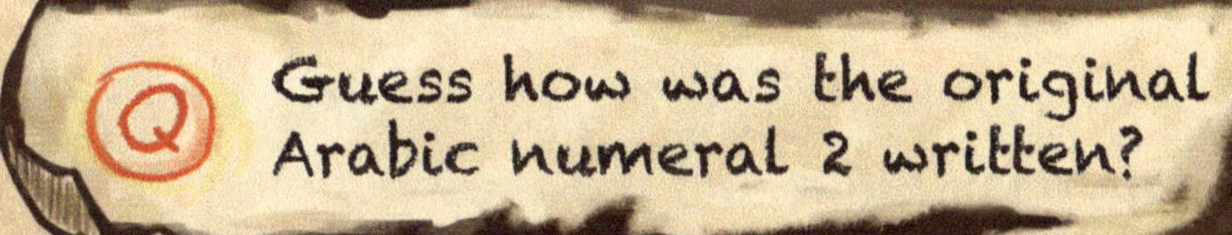

Knowledge Map

Maya

Although the Mayans understood the place value system, they used the **base-20 system**, using **3** symbols: 0 (shell-shaped symbol), 1 (dot), and 5 (horizontal line) to represent numbers in combinations.

P. 40

Ancient Rome

Ancient Romans used only **7** basic symbols for counting but dealing with slightly larger numbers became problematic without understanding digits.

P. 66

Ancient Babylonians also knew the place value system but used a **base-60 system**, with a wedge-shaped cuneiform "𒁹" representing 1 and another wedge-shaped cuneiform "𒌋" representing 10, showing numbers through their combinations.

P. 54

Chinese counting rods used only **one type of small stick**, placed horizontally and vertically, combined to represent any natural number in a **base-10 system**, which is an ingenious counting method!

P. 78

Equipment Introduction

Capacity: 500 ml (a little more than a quart)

Bottle cap with sealing design to prevent leaks

Can be rolled up for easy carrying

Foldable bottle

Reusable and eco-friendly material

Can be charged or used batteries

Medallion-like flashlight

5 cm

Press

Clockwise

Counter-clockwise

Size: 5cm (about 2 in.) in diameter

Rotate to adjust the brightness

Simulated gill

Breathing mouthpiece

Fish fin converter

(can convert to liquid air)

Fish-eye lamp

Beam angle up to 180°

Substantial light beam distance up to 300 m (about 984 ft.)

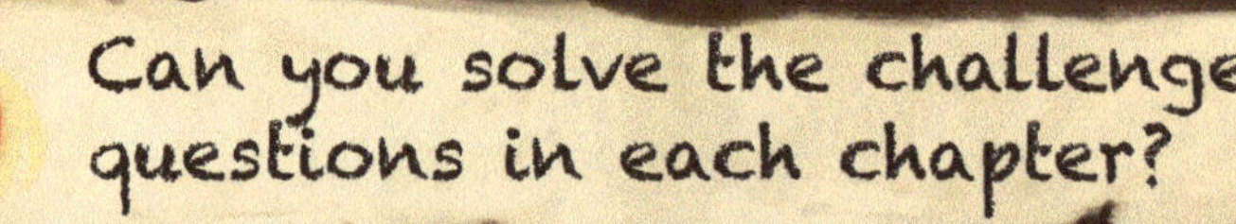

Challenge	Answer
Challenge 1	
Challenge 2	D
Challenge 3	1233246
Challenge 4	100
Challenge 5	123
Challenge 6	LXVII
Challenge 7	2222
Challenge 8	Z

MATH STAR

5

1

XL